PLAY
WholEarth Game

A Game of Trust & Sharing

Alanson Jared Charles

Nathan Hassall

Illustrations by Rachel Kraft

NEWMAN SPRINGS PUBLISHING
320 Broad Street
Red Bank, NJ 07701

First originally published by Newman Springs Publishing 2019

ISBN 978-1-64096-964-3 (Paperback)
ISBN 978-1-64096-965-0 (Digital)

Printed in the United States of America

To all those yet to come.
Pay it forward, buy it back.
Together WeCan Seed What Happens Next.
For every living thing, just five things.
We, depends on unity.

Contents

Introduction

Welcome all you free thinkers and rule breakers. You
can't stand rules because in your heart you know
there's a better way. You've found your tribe.
>—Garret LoPorto, *Wayseers Manifesto*

If you're reading this, you're probably already one of the key players. You have taken the red pill; there is no going back. We are in the grip of a progressive illness, and we stand at the turning point. We came all this way just to find each other. Together we can seed what happens next.

Half measures will avail nothing. On a planet that is estimated to be 4.8 billion years old, it is almost impossible to fully comprehend that in just 200 years we have ravaged our Mother Earth, *Gaia*. Any child that turns on its mother is in great confusion. How many times have we played the WholEarth Game? How many times have we come from behind to win this game? After billions of years practicing, we should be pretty good at it by now.

What have we done?

We are like all creatures. We are drawn to the light scientifically and magnetically. It is impossible to fight against this light.

Imagine we are on the Spaceship Enterprise One WholEarth.

Our vessel is travelling around a star we call our sun. This is just a small spark of the galactic sun at the center of our galaxy. We are moving around our sun in time and space at 60,000 miles per hour. Our star travels around the sun of the center at 45,000 miles per hour. We are in constant movement.

Here we are again—3 minutes of stoppage time, 3 goals down—to take back what is rightfully ours.

All hands on deck!

Everybody Plays at Practice

Practice, Practice, Practice!

Find joy in practicing what you love.

The WholEarth Game

There are games that end and games that don't end. In the game we have been born into the rules are fixed and rigid. In the "WholEarth Game" the rules change to keep the game going.

If you have decided to play the WholEarth Game you are ready to answer YES or NO to 5 simple questions.

The WholEarth Game is inspired by the World Game—an invention by Richard Buckminster Fuller, better known as Bucky—on how to "Make the world work, for 100% of humanity, and all living things in the shortest possible time, through spontaneous cooperation, without ecological offense or the disadvantage of anyone." However, when Buckminster Fuller proposed the World Game in 1961, the technology did not exist to implement his vision. Step in today's world.

The five components are the seeds of the game. These allow us to achieve two things: to live and travel without harm to ourselves or the planet. This allows us to be the best people we can be which will in turn allow us to be the best team players. The whole purpose of this life on planet earth is to clean up all our existing mistakes to allow our species to live well on this third rock from the sun.

This planet provides the five essential elements needed to sustain life for countless galaxies of living things. These five components should be provided free of charge.

Do you have…?

1. A safe place to sleep tonight?
2. Access to clean pure drinking water everywhere?
3. Delicious healthy organic food to eat?

4. Energy you need to be happy, joyful, and free?
5. Are you willing to help others?

But wait everything provided by Mother Eartha Gaia now costs money. We have been forced to slave at jobs we hate in order to buy the things we need. That's not fair! How did we let them do this to us?

The WholEarth Game was created to help us figure out how to get just five things to all living things.

Remember everybody plays at practice.

Just imagine we are playing a *real* video game and we have unlimited restarts. Most good players—like you—will play a game over and over until they achieve the next level. Our goal is to find ways to live and travel without harm, and to help others to live and travel without harm on One WholEarth.

Let the Game begin.

The Game of Trust and Sharing

The purpose of the WholEarth Game is to get you to think about—and consequently understand—that you *do* have significant ecological choices and the power to enforce them. There is a concerted global effort afoot in our society that is focused on the complete destruction of our environment. We, "WholEarth," depends on unity." Join the WholEarth team and do one small thing each day for the planet that is still sick. What is the greatest good for the least amount of effort?

Soccer is the World's Game. Soccer describes the WholEarth game too. The most famous team that utilizes these principles is the 2017–18 *La Liga* (Spanish Premier League) champions, Barcelona. They are able to make fifty or more pass connections. They know where everyone is, and they trust each other's abilities and keep the ball, the object of desire, from the other team. Without trust, you are likely to spend time chasing the object of desire. The Ball. We cannot have One WholEarth without trust.

Everybody plays the WholEarth Game. We're all on the same team, the laws of the universe apply to all living things equally. This is the game of life.

The goal of a successful coach is to teach a set of skills needed by each player. They are the tools needed to slow time, avoid panic, and make good decisions. A good pass is kind and gentle, able to be received without losing control. Practicing these skills will instill certain values that can be used as a philosophy throughout life. This can include trusting one's own ability, working together as a team, sharing success and failure, developing compassion and sportsmanship, respect for opposing players, winning gracefully, and losing graciously. This is why soccer (or more accurately, football) is the world's game. These are just some of the values that can be taught and learned. In the context of a game, all players, even opposing players, cooperate within the framework of the game. Therefore, no matter what team you happen to be on, there is always a common agreement about the rules. The WholEarth Game also has rules that we must agree on.

In soccer, it takes a unified effort to score a goal. It also takes a unified team effort to keep the other team from scoring. True sportspeople don't let petty differences affect the true value of their game. They play as a unit for the benefit of the team. Anything short of that will not create a successful team. The true spirit of sportsmanship is fundamental.

So we who play the WholEarth game want to score goals and win. We want to maintain possession of the earth and advance it into a future of plenty. We want to penetrate with mobility and depth those who would stand in our way—with width and creativity—to beat the ego and choose life. Then we want to prevent the other team from scoring by prevention, delaying their advances, and regaining possession of the earth. We want to play this game with concentration, composure, togetherness, and forgiveness.

Use the skills of the WholEarth Game to slow down time. Make good decisions. There is only one way to go and that's towards the goal.

There are two competing games—games that end and games that don't end. In the first game the rules are fixed and rigid. In the second, the rules change whenever necessary to keep the game going. These are also known as the finite game and infinite game.

Those who play the finite game are called business, banking, war, Wall Street, politics as usual, and our lust for gold. Those who play the infinite game are called potlatch, *tiyóspaye*, family, samba, those who pray, tree planters, tree huggers, storytellers, and truth speakers. People trying to keep the game going are activists, artivists, actionists, actionistas, conservationists, librarians, teachers, agitators, and organizers.

The approach is concerned with the whole earth, the entire history of the planet, and all of humanity—both living now and those yet to be born. The tribe is only as strong as its weakest link.

See you at practice.

R. Buckminster Fuller

Captain Spaceship Earth

My inspiration for the WholEarth Game stems directly from Buckminster Fuller in what he called the World Game. If we use his Dymaxion map, we can see the world from a different perspective. We can see a path to quickly restore the planet for the benefit of all living things in the shortest amount of time imaginable.

Richard Buckminster Fuller was one of the key innovators of the twentieth century. Born July 12, 1895, he passed on July 1, 1983. During his almost one hundred years on this planet, he was probably one of the most popular futurists and global thinkers to consider the welfare and benefit of global life for all. It was he who coined the term *spaceship earth* and was known as an architect, thinker, mathematician, philosopher, visionary, poet, and cosmologist. In many ways, he paved the road ahead for those that followed.

One of the most important things he worked on and tried to get accepted worldwide was what he called *comprehensive anticipatory design science*. This was a challenge to foresee and resolve humanity's main problems by giving "more and more life support for everybody, with less and less resources." This partly stemmed from the death of his four-year-old daughter which he blamed this on poor or inadequate housing conditions. He made it his life purpose to invent solutions to remedy poor housing conditions worldwide.

One of his more telling comments about his position was:

> For the first time in history it is now possible to take care of everybody at a higher standard of living than any have ever known. Only ten years ago the 'more with less' technology reached the point where this could be done. All humanity now has the option of becoming enduringly successful.

Fuller believed strongly in the creative abilities of mankind and believed they were limitless. He also felt the use of these abilities in the development of technology and design-led solutions would provide a positive future for all. He also said,

> I do know that technologically humanity now has the opportunity, for the first time in its history, to operate our planet in such a manner as to support and accommodate all humanity at a substantially more advanced standard of living than any humans have ever experienced.

Fuller led an interesting life and was innovative in countless projects, all designed to increase the standard of living across the world. He believed technology was the way to solve the myriad of problems and was instrumental in creating a number of those technologies himself. He is the one who created the geodesic dome, a revolutionary house designed for ecologically efficient housing for the mass market. It was made of lightweight materials and has a high strength to weight ratio. This was designed in the 1940s, way ahead of its time. It was designed with a series of triangles which could be replicated anywhere in the world using recycled materials for very little cost.

Buckminster Fuller was not college educated; in fact, he was the first member of his family for over a century that failed to graduate from Harvard University. He received no formal training in engineering or structural mechanics but taught himself while in the Navy during the Second World War. He was perpetually concerned that humanity was on the road to extinction. He stated in an interview in 1978:

> Nature is trying very hard to make us succeed, but nature does not depend on us. We are not the only experiment.

Although against the mainstream system of teaching which focuses on learning enough to get a job and become *productive in society*, he did believe strongly in educating people, stating:

> The true business of people should be to go back to school and think about whatever it was they were thinking about before somebody came along and told them they had to earn a living.
> And:
> Quite clearly, our task is predominantly metaphysical, for it is how to get all of humanity to educate itself swiftly enough to generate spontaneous social behaviors that will avoid extinction.

Buckminster Fuller was a seer, if you will, who tried to educate people to the catastrophe the planet had been heading toward since the beginning of the Industrial Revolution. What we now find happening to our ecosystem was forewarned by Fuller, who laid the groundwork for others who continue where he left off.

Our *spaceship earth* has been traveling for billions of years and will continue to travel whether humans are riding it or not. His contribution was fundamental in learning how to right *spaceship earth*, and he knew exactly what should be followed and expanded this to all facets of existence.

Fuller's dedication and life spent in the research and elucidation of what we are now faced with should be lauded and incorporated into our daily life. The poisons being dumped into the ecosystem daily are overwhelming nature's ability to purify herself. She needs help. Anyone who wants to become active in assisting the planet's healing process should first, without fail, examine the lessons learned by this incredible individual and use his great knowledge as the basis of building a new world.

Fuller challenges everyone to learn and make a difference. He was a firm believer in the single voice: that one entity could affect great change in a world where *specialization* has ruined the ability to think clearly and effectively in the *whole world concept*. He said in his book, *No More Secondhand God* (1963):

> On first priority in design consideration
> is the full realization of individual potential in
> order to reach the second derivative—full realiza-
> tion for all individuals.

With all that this man has done, I leave you with this profound thought, another one of his pieces of insight:

The opposite of nature is impossible.

For Every Living Thing,
Just 5 Things

Because it's the right thing to do!

Basic living at Boulder Garden. 2010.

The Home

The house, the body, the planet.

New energy-efficient homes built using healthy natural materials with the most advanced technology available will save energy and reduce carbon. Modernizing existing homes is our priority. Optimizing all existing buildings is essential.

The home is complete when all five elements are equally present. The WholEarth home is inspired by nature.

The WholEarth home is designed and built to the highest level of safe, clean technology. Water will be collected and used to the highest benefit of living things that contribute to everyone's health and well-being. Food comes from the garden to the kitchen as part of the WholEarth home. Energy is provided by clean solar power and wind and stored for use as needed.

Our occupation is to live a healthy beneficial life in the best, most energy-efficient designs. Using nature as a guide, all our designs will follow the same basic program: the heart will be at the center. The living room and the kitchen are the home's heart because the hearth and fire are the energy center.

Our life is a pattern. Each day, we leave and come back home. Each day, we are together with our families, then we separate from them, and then we come together again. We go to school or work, but we usually return for dinner to watch TV or read in our comfortable clothes. We play this *game* day after day.

Where do I begin to talk about home? We all share a longing to find it. And for many of us, it is not complete without way too much space within four walls in some neighborhood that seems to be arranged in concentration camps. And they are a type of concentrated sprawl of one poor design after another. Years ago, I saw the ludicrous nature of the building system of the great American Dream. The white picket fence around the *dream* that was the modern castle.

In the last couple of years, I have met and gotten to know people who see their home as the great outdoors. I spent a year on a friends ranch. When I was there, I trained myself to be comfortable sleeping outdoors. It was there that I truly found my place here on spaceship earth.

Christopher Alexander

The Timeless Way of Building.

The Tao of building. If we follow the timeless way, we will guarantee the highest quality of life you can imagine.

Christopher Wolfgang Alexander was born in Vienna, Austria, on October 4, 1936. He is most known for his architectural design theory, which states that users of a structure know more about what they need in a building than an architect does. He designed, along with Sarah Ishikawa and Murray Silverstein, *pattern language*. This language allows anyone to design and build a building of any scale. He carries a bachelor's degree in architecture, a master's degree in mathematics, and he received the first PhD in architecture from Harvard University ever awarded.

For over thirty years, Alexander researched, wrote, and contemplated modern architectural design methods and concluded that there is something fundamentally wrong with them. His biggest contention is that modern methods fail in their basic design and engineering to improve the human condition. He cites the problems as:

- The lack of ability to balance individual societal, group, and ecological needs.

- The absence of purpose, order, and human scale.
- Functional and visual failure in adjusting to native physical and social environments.
- The construction of artifacts that people don't like.
- The developmental growth of materials and their inconsistent use of uniform components when they are applied specifically.

In his book *The Timeless Way of Building* (1979), he states one of the main themes behind his thoughts on building for the human condition as:

> There is one timeless way of building. It is a thousand years old, and the same today as it has ever been. The great traditional buildings of the past, the villages and tents and temples in which man feels at home, have always been made by people who were very close to the center of this way. It is not possible to make great buildings, or great towns, beautiful places, places where you feel yourself, places where you feel alive, except by following this way. And, as you will see, this way will lead anyone who looks for it to buildings which are themselves as ancient in their form, as the trees and hills, and as our faces are.

This exemplifies his belief that those who live in the center of buildings, their homes, lodges, community centers, etc. understand better what fits in with their life and what is more harmonious to their lifestyle than any modern architect could design. Many of his ideas stemmed from his observations that most medieval cities were harmonious and attractive. He stated that this was because, "They were built to local regulations that required specific features but freed the architect to adapt them to particular situations."

Alexander has had several works built, most notably, the Eishin Campus near Tokyo, the West Dean Visitors Centre in West

Sussex, England, the Julian Street Inn (homeless shelter) in San Jose, California, the Martinez House (an experimental house made of lightweight concrete) in Martinez, California, low cost housing in Mexicali, Mexico, and several private houses. His work is characterized by a special quality, as he calls it: *the quality without name*, that encourages feelings of belonging to the place and structure. This is very similar to the feelings people have toward their city's historic buildings and urban spaces and was precisely what Alexander was trying to capture with his design theories.

Alexander and his colleagues at the Center for Environmental Structure are building a movement and a movement which in their words, "Lays the basis for an entirely new approach to architecture, building and planning, which will replace existing ideas and practices entirely."

When looking at the beautiful cities of the world those that were built hundreds of years ago, it is critically important to note that they were not designed and made by architects but by the people. It is to this unity and harmony that Alexander has focused his theories and energy on to propagate his movement.

Paolo Soleri

Archologist

The future of architecture is archology which combines architecture with ecology.

There is no other direction we can take.

Imagine combing "Archology" and the Timeless Way.

Paolo Soleri was born in Italy in the town of Turin on June 21, 1919. He received his PhD in architecture from Politecnico di Torino in 1946 with highest honors at just twenty-seven years old. In 1947, he spent a year and a half in the United States in a fellowship with Frank Lloyd Wright. He gained international respect for a bridge design he displayed at the Museum of Modern Art and for being published in *The Architecture of Bridges* by Elizabeth Mock.

When he returned to Italy, he was commissioned to build a ceramics factory called the Ceramica Artistica Solimene. With his new designs in the ceramic industry, he created new strategies that paved the way to fund and support his theoretical work. He resettled to Scottsdale, Arizona, in 1956 with his wife and two daughters and established the nonprofit Cosanti Foundation.

This foundation was setup primarily for Soleri to test his theory and project named Arcosanti. This project was to design a town for a population of 5,000 where the environmental impact would be minimal. Soleri had a concept he called arcology which was architecture coherent with ecology. It was his intention to introduce a city, or cities, that were designed to be more efficient by diminishing the use of energy, raw materials, and land, reducing waste and environmental pollution.

This community—located near Cordes Junction, roughly seventy miles north of Phoenix—has been under construction since 1970. Basically, Soleri's concept is to design living areas where they can become totally self-sufficient and have the least amount of impact on the world around it. By utilizing his principles, a city could theoretically support itself when operated in unity and working with the built-in advantages that nature provides. This would maximize human interaction by uniting them in a collective effort to support the whole.

An exhibition in Washington, D.C., organized in 1970 by the Corcoran Gallery of Art was called The Architectural Visions of Paolo Soleri. This exhibition traveled throughout the United States and Canada and broke records for attendance. In 1976, another exhibit opened in the Xerox Square Center in Rochester, New York. This one was titled Two Suns Arcology: A Concept for Future Cities. Another in 1989 at the New York Academy of Sciences was titled Paolo Soleri Habitats: Ecologic Minutiae. His latest exhibition was Soleri's Cities: Architecture for Planet Earth and Beyond and was featured at the Scottsdale Center for the Arts in Scottsdale, Arizona. His work has been seen worldwide.

Although Soleri has received numerous awards and medals, his focus has always been on designing a city to fulfill his dream of self-sufficiency. It was his strongest conviction that humans can live on planet earth harmoniously with a symbiotic relationship to nature. He desired to reduce impact on the environment and establish a functioning set of values based on the timeless way of building. As a visionary, Soleri is a lighthouse of encouragement and inspiration. The minute I discovered his work, I was overjoyed that a real solution was possible.

Water

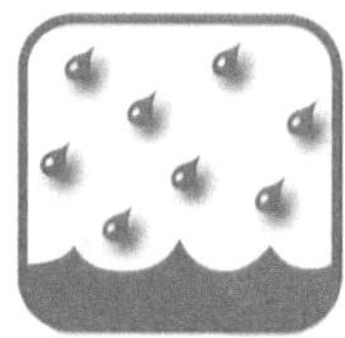

Water. It is the right of every living thing to enjoy fresh clean water, isn't it?

In 1996, ecological engineering was an emerging field capable of addressing a broad range of issues. It was intended to influence the future of waste treatment, environmental restoration and remediation, food production, fuel generation, architecture, and the design of human settlements. Ecology is the long-term intellectual foundation for the development of new technologies to support life and society.

The WholEarth system uses this as a primary element of sustainable whole systems design. The future of life on this planet depends upon the availability of clean, fresh water.

Of all the discovered planets, we are the only one known to support life and it is due in large part to this precious resource. For this reason, water is the most important element of the WholEarth building system.

We say, "Use less, waste none."

We must be committed to designing homes and communities that will use water as many times as possible before returning it to nature as pure as when it came to us.

Water will never be more important than it is right now.

John Todd

Living Machinist

John Todd is a biologist who works in a field that is referred to as *the general field of ecological design*, and his concepts are often what becomes the basis of alternative technologies in their application. Born in Hamilton, Ontario, Canada, in 1939, Todd has focused his professional interests on solving the problems of waste water processing and food production. Todd also created an ecological design mandala with the issues we're facing today and his suggested solutions to solve those same problems.

Todd and his wife Nancy cofounded the New Alchemy Institute in 1969 to carry out basic research in aspects of biology in order to apply biological science to technology. He and his colleagues designed miniature ecosystems that were mainly self-perpetuating and, therefore, brought these principles into the realm of human needs.

In turn, while working on the principles of design for food producing systems, it led to pioneering new methods of treating sewage and industrial waste water. His method used microorganisms, plants, and fish by application.

With the help of his colleagues, Todd developed what were referred to as *living machines*. This was environmentally-engineered technology to conserve, restore, or reconcile sewage or other polluted water by mimicking and speeding up the natural purification process of marshes, ponds, and streams. In application, it is a self-sustaining system that treats a specific section of water using the doctrines of ecological engineering. It creates varied populations of bacteria and other microorganisms, plants, trees, fish, snails, algae, and other living creatures.

Living Machines are essential to quickly repairing our local immediate ecosystems. A living Machine for every building and on every corner will be required in the future. A Living Machine by any name will quickly begin to heal *Gaia*.

Todd has been working for over thirty years on his designs and redesigning when necessary to bring humanity and ecology together to form a successful working relationship. As he states:

> We have spent ninety-nine percent of our history in the wild, sky, water, and trees are embedded in us. Sever that and we've severed what it is to be human.

In May of 2008, Todd was the first winner and recipient of the First Annual Buckminster Fuller Challenge. According to the Buckminster Fuller Institute:

> Dr. John Todd's comprehensive design strategy to bring about a carbon neutral world, in the opinion of this jury, best embodies the bold, visionary approach to large scale societal transformation pioneered by Buckminster Fuller. Dr. Todd's proposal sets forth a profound vision to heal the environmental and economic scars of the Appalachian region and a detailed strategy to build a dynamic sustainable economic basis for lasting renewal.

Currently Todd is involved in trying to create what he calls Ecological Malls where people can produce food and energy and recycle waste in a biologically driven loop. He states, "I want to graft small farms and recycling and maybe have a rain forest exhibit and a butterfly park." He teaches Ecological Design at the University of Vermont, and one of his course requirements is for his students to help him fulfill his dream.

All these procedures, the water flow design and ecological relationships for the operation of these projects, have already been worked out and are well-known. What isn't as well-known is how to put them all together into a long-term process of workability. As Todd said, "I started as a scientist. Now I feel I am becoming an artist assembling scientific ideals like a painter assembles colors on a canvas." The pictures that can be painted by using his ecological systems are nothing less than miraculous.

Here is the course he taught that will allow you to see a future that is ready to blossom at any time.

Food

Food is free if you grow it yourself. Every WholEarth home grows its own food.

Food is the natural by-product of clean and living water. We are living things, and we are part of this biosphere. We need to remain constantly vigilant of our place as members of this great society. This includes all other living entities. But over the last few hundred years, our species has become arrogant and wasteful, and the industrialized world has pulled us away from the place where we live.

In less than one hundred years, we have nearly depleted all of earth's natural resources. Anything we could use for our own benefit has been taken without any concern for our fellow life-forms, and we now jeopardize our very existence on this planet.

The energy used to produce and transport food is among the highest percentage of the cause of global warming. The best way to reduce carbon is to grow as much food as possible as close to the home and community as possible.

The health benefits of eating local seasonal food are just now being realized. The concept of WholEarth is that community farms will provide most of what is consumed by its residents. The partnership of the agricultural craftsperson with the culinary craftsperson can only enhance the quality of life.

Imagine homes and communities with people for the environment. By practicing biodynamics, organic farming, and permaculture, we will benefit in the long run.

Masanobu Fukuoka

The One Straw Revolutionary

I do not particularly like the word 'work.' Human beings are the only animals who have to work, and I think that is the most ridiculous thing in the world. Other animals make their livings by living, but people work like crazy, thinking that they have to in order to stay alive. The bigger the job, the greater the challenge, the more wonderful they think it is. It would be good to give up that way of thinking and live an easy, comfortable life with plenty of free time. I think that the way animals live in the tropics, stepping outside in the morning and evening to see if there is something to eat, and taking a long nap in the afternoon, must be a wonderful life. For human beings, a life of such simplicity would be possible if one worked to produce directly his daily necessities. In such a life, work is not work as people generally think of it, but simply doing what needs to be done.

Fukuoka lived from 1913–2008. He was a Japanese philosopher and farmer known for his natural farming methods. He looked at indigenous cultures to create a zero-herbicide grain cultivation farming method. From this, he developed a farming method which needed the least amount of work often referred to as *natural farming* and sometimes referred to as *do-nothing farming*.

> In my opinion, if 100 percent of the people were farming it would be ideal. If each person were given one quarter-acre, that is 1 1/4 acres to a family of five, that would be more than enough land to support the family for the whole year. If natural farming were practiced, a farmer would also have plenty of time for leisure and social activities within the village community. I think this is the most direct path toward making this country a happy, pleasant land.

Fukuoka wrote a significant number of books and contributed to scientific papers. He was not only interested in food but he also wanted to inspire people to eat natural food and alter their lifestyles. He was committed to teaching the value of respecting the principles of nature.

As for education, Fukuoka attended the Gifu Prefecture Agricultural College where he was initially trained as a microbiologist and later became a specialist in plant pathology. In 1937, Fukuoka was hospitalized with pneumonia, during which he had such a powerful experience, his worldview entirely changed. This experience ultimately made him doubt the effectiveness of the West's agricultural science and led him to quit his job as a research scientist and return to his family's farm.

Fukuoka then started to experiment on the farmland and implement different techniques on organic citrus orchids. He believed that his methods allowed him to see the vast difference between human nonintervention and nature.

After the Second World War, Fukuoka had lost a significant amount of his family's lands because of the American redistribution policies. However, in 1947 he implemented natural farming again on the smaller bits of lands in order to grow rice and barley. From there, he wrote his first ever book, called *Mu 1: The God Revolution.*

> When it is understood that one loses joy
> and happiness in the attempt to possess them,
> the essence of natural farming will be realized.
> The ultimate goal of farming is not the growing
> of crops, but the cultivation and perfection of
> human beings.

In 1979 onwards, Fukuoka went across the globe to give lectures, plant seeds directly, and grow crops in areas that had not grown anything for years. He received many awards in a multitude of countries that recognized his achievements. By the 1980s, Fukuoka managed to ship ninety tons of citrus to Tokyo every year.

In 1983, Fukuoka went to Europe for fifty days to provide workshops and teach farmers how to sow seeds. He went to Somalia and Ethiopia in 1985 in order to revegetate the desert and help villages and refugee camps. He then travelled back to the United States where he gave international conferences on natural farming. He also went to farms, cities, and even forests to both provide lectures and talk to the public.

After visiting many countries to teach natural farming including Thailand, Tanzania, Philippines, Greece, Spain, China, and India, Fukuoka finally resettled in Japan.

On 16 August 2008, Fukuoka died at the age of 95.

Geoff Lawton

The Food Forester

"You can solve all the world's problems in a garden."

Australian Geoff Lawton is a renowned designer, teacher, speaker, and permaculture consultant. He is a specialist in permaculture and community development.

Beginning in 1985, Lawton has assumed a variety of roles and jobs ranging from designing, teaching, and consulting and has worked in over thirty countries worldwide. He works with clients from a variety of backgrounds: from individuals, to governments, to multinational businesses.

One of Lawton's predominant endeavors is to produce and establish self-duplicating educational demonstration sites. During his lifetime, he has already taught over 15,000 students across the globe in permaculture.

However, Lawton's grand plan is to get a replication of aid projects as quickly as possible in order to combat the ever increasing food and water crisis.

> Nature demands a gift for everything that it
> gives, so what we have to keep doing, is return-
> ing [leaves and compost materials] back to the
> soil, then we're continuously giving the gifts to
> nature, because we have a return cycle.

Lawton's continual dedication to permaculture across the world has not gone unrecognized. In 1996, Lawton was given the Permaculture Community Services Award for his work in Australia and around the globe.

When Bill Mollison retired in 1997, he requested Lawton establish a Permaculture Research Institute on Tagari Farm in Tasmania. Lawton advanced the site across the span of three years and further established The Permaculture Research Institute (PRI) Australia. It was later moved to Zaytuna farm where it still exists.

Lawton is currently the managing director of PRI Australia as well as the PRI USA, and both are nonprofit organizations.

Lawton and Mollison have collectively hosted and taught a variety of courses together, and Lawton presents on one of Mollision's DVDs. Lawton makes an appearance in John D. Liu's documentary *Hope in a Changing Climate* and also appears at a TEDx conference in the United Arab Emirates.

More recently, Lawton has been able to stabilize a permaculture ecosystem in Jordan as well as a land restoration program in Saudi Arabia.

> Your own imagination as to the true ability
> of the permaculture design system, you need to
> t rust the system and stick to mainframe basics
> with profound and thorough thinking while
> trusting yourself.

Energy

Everything is energy; we are all connected. The universe is electric.

Energy: sun, wind, water, and gravity can provide all the electricity we will ever need. It is now simply a matter of making the decision to invest in and create the solution. In a large building, the combination of all these natural elements would create a surplus of usable potential.

At WholEarth, we build homes and communities with people who are concerned for the environment. This means that we blend our homes and communities into the local ecosystems whenever possible. This means building our homes into the landscape whenever possible.

We will use fewer natural resources and make them last as long as possible. The homes we build are meant to last; they use less energy and supply much of their own energy by using safe, long-lasting solar or wind energy.

Our designs are inspired by nature. We use natural, healthy materials in order to assist you in living a long and healthy life. We hope this will encourage you to live your life with more awareness. Our designs are like pebbles dropped in a lake sending positive ripples outwards, bringing us back to a place of harmony within our surroundings.

Nikola Tesla

The Master of Energy

On the stroke of midnight between July 9 and 10, 1856, a fierce electrical storm raged. Who was born that day? None other than Nikola Tesla.

Tesla was a mechanical engineer, physicist, inventor, and futurist. His philosophical approach led him to a host of fundamental insights and inventions. In his words,

> One must be sane to think clearly, but one
> can think deeply and be quite insane.

When Tesla got older, he played with energy in a way that most people would play with toys. He was able to conceptualize and visualize ideas in his mind and was able to build them without meticulous planning.

He was the master of lightning, working on electromagnetism with Thomas Edison which created the foundation for technologies such as the modern radio. He also postulated utilizing the hydroelectric power of the Niagara Falls which is used today as a source of generating energy.

Tesla's incredible legacy has been further used in a variety of electronic items we use—and taken for granted—everyday including remote controls and cell phones. His discoveries also led to technologies such as radar, X-rays, and, unfortunately, guided missiles.

In 1931, at the height of his career, Tesla made the cover of *Time Magazine*. He also boasted an impressive array of friends ranging from Mark Twain to J. P. Morgan.

Most importantly, Tesla was willing to give his life to inventions so that he could improve life for all humanity. He dreamed of giving the world free energy. It's now time to realize his dream!

Tesla has taught me about how modest conceptual ideas can eventually affect whole generations in both the present and the future. To realize the dreams that I've conjured would be to do justice to this great thinker. In his words,

> The spread of civilization may be likened to
> a fire; first, a feeble spark, next a flickering flame,
> then a mighty blaze, ever increasing in speed and
> power.

I endeavor to use his *spark* to give us the chance to make our planet a place for all life-forms.

Occupation

Everyone on Spaceship One WholEarth has a full-time job: to stay focused and help others to stay focused.

The infinite game goes on forever. We just have to follow the principles of *Natural Capitalism*. And have fun.

We all have a job. Our job is to ask questions and find answers. Our job is to work each day to keep this planet going and giving to our next generation and all living things. If we all do one small thing each day to cure ourselves from this carbon addiction, we can find happiness, joy, and freedom. Then we will have a great place to live, clean water to drink, great food to eat, an abundance of clean energy, and time to enjoy our lives with our family and friends.

Every living thing is involved with some form of occupation, from a single-celled organism to a complex human being. It is against our nature to be deprived of the ability to contribute to the quality of our own lives.

With scarce resources or limited access to funds and individual freedom, what every other living thing does so naturally was used to control some people by others.

Simply put, occupation is what all living things do to live. Your hobbies, pastimes, raising of a family, athletic activities, and career are all included. Your pattern of life is what we design for. WholEarth includes all of life's activities in our description of occupation.

The WholEarth Development Corporation is here to design the structures needed for us all to live healthy lives.

Amory Lovins

Natural Capitalist

The WholEarth Game would not be possible without the work of this man. Because he did, I know we can.

Amory Bloch Lovins was born in Washington, D.C. on November 13, 1947, and he spent most of his youth in Maryland and Massachusetts. After spending time abroad going to college in England and receiving his master of arts, he relocated to western Colorado in 1982. He has received ten honorary doctorates and numerous awards. He has published twenty-nine books and in 2009, *Time magazine* named him as one of the World's 100 Most Influential People.

Lovins has been an optimistic environmentalist since the early 1970s and strongly supports the use of *soft energy paths*. He promotes energy efficiency and the use of renewable energy sources. He also states that the production of energy should be done at or near the area where the energy is actually used.

Lovins and his wife, L. Hunter, established the Rocky Mountain Institute in 1982 in Snowmass, Colorado. Their focus, along with their colleagues, is to nurture proficient resource use and sustainable development.

Lovins's soft energy path refers to energy efficiency regarding the use of soft energy technologies which include solar, biofuel, geothermal, and wind technologies. The output would match the demand required for their use. Solar energy use on houses is a key example of a soft energy technology and is fundamental to a soft energy strategy.

At the Rocky Mountain Institute, Lovins developed the concept of what he calls the hypercar. It is built with ultralight construction and using an aerodynamic body with advanced composite materials and a hybrid drive. The designers of the car state it will achieve a three to five times improvement in fuel economy with at least as good—if not better—performance, safety, and cost compared with the cars of today.

Lovins has spent most of his professional life advocating the use of energy in a sustainable way. He has sought to implement a way to use low impact energy—such as his soft energy technologies—to create a financially sound incentive to use soft energy.

Most people are unaware or are working for a company with no vested interest in energy savings, that by using what Lovins calls a Negawatt Revolution which is a rapid deployment of energy-saving technology, such as L.E.D.s (Light Emitting Diode), so that the imprint on the world's ecology will be minimized.

Probably one of the more well-known concepts that Lovins has created is his interpretation and creation of what he calls *Natural Capitalism*. It is defined by the four principles he has determined.

The Four Principles of Natural Capitalism:

1. Radical resource productivity: Using natural resources far more efficiently is both profitable and better for the environment.
2. Biomimicry: Using nature as a model and measure yields superior design solutions that profitably eliminate waste, loss, and harm. Nature offers extraordinary design solutions honed by 4.8 billion years of rigorous testing; what-

ever did not work was recalled by the Manufacturer, Planet Earth.

3. Service and flow economy: Providing appropriate services in place of direct product consumption—decreasing cost of travel and material waste. The concept entails a new perception of value, a shift from the acquisition of goods as a measure of affluence to an economy where the continuous receipt of quality, utility, and performance promotes well-being.

4. Reinvestment in natural capital: Sustaining, restoring, and expanding stocks of natural capital will help reverse worldwide planetary destruction, so that the biosphere can produce more abundant ecosystem services and natural resources.

Lovins also argued that in addition to environmental benefits, global political stresses can be lowered by Western nations committing to the soft energy path. He believes that the soft path impacts are *gentle, pleasant, and manageable.* The positive impacts can range from the individual and household level to those affecting the very fabric of society at the national and international level.

Paul Hawken

Non Profit

Paul Hawken was born in California on February 8, 1946 and is an author, entrepreneur, and environmentalist. He didn't get a formal degree but spent time at UC Berkeley and San Francisco State University. He also worked in the Civil Rights Movement. He has written seven books with four of them becoming national bestsellers. One of the bestsellers he wrote was called *Blessed Unrest*.

Hawken is also responsible for producing and hosting a seventeen-part PBS television show—*Growing a Business*—that was aired in 115 countries and seen by over one hundred million people. He also founded the Natural Capital Institute located in Sausalito, California. This institute created WiserEarth, an open-source networking platform linking NGOs, businesses, government, foundations, students, organizers, social entrepreneurs, activists, scientists, academics, and any citizen troubled by social injustice and environmental problems.

Hawken also started up one of the first natural food companies that used only agriculture-grown with sustainable methods. He is currently the head of OneSun, LLC—an energy company focusing on extremely low-cost solar energy based on green chemistry and biomimicry and Highwater Global. Highwater Global is an impact fund that uses the highest standards of corporate ethical, social, and environmental conduct.

In *Blessed Unrest*, Hawken argues a vast world changing movement is coming and calls it a *movement with no name.* He believes this will prevail and thinks of this movement as what is and what is not humane as opposed to being developed by ideology.

He further expresses his feeling of this movement by stating:

> It is axiomatic that we are at a threshold in human existence, a fundamental change in understanding about our relationship to nature and each other. We are moving from a world created by privilege to a world created by community. The current thrust of history is too supple to be labeled, but global themes are emerging in response to cascading ecological crises and human suffering. These ideas include the need for radical social change, the reinvention of market-based economics, the empowerment of women, activism on all levels, and the need for localized economic control. There are insistent calls for autonomy, appeals for a new resource ethic based on the tradition of the commons, demands for the reinstatement of cultural primacy over corporate hegemony, and a rising demand for radical transparency in politics and corporate decision making. It has been said that environmentalism failed as a movement, or worse yet, died. It is the other way around. Everyone on earth will be an environmentalist in the not too distant future, driven there by necessity and experience.

In 2002, *Fortune* called Hawken "The original hippie entrepreneur." He was the merchant of Marin County who ventured into business when others were dropping out. Today Hawken occupies a unique niche in the American landscape combining bottom-line business credentials (he regularly addresses corporate audiences) with credibility among environmentalists and social critics.

He once wrote, and stands by, the following sentence: "There is no polite way to say that business is destroying the world." Yet he also believes, passionately, that business—with its restless energy, imagination, and creativity—will one day get us out of the mess it has made. Hawken states: "I believe business is on the verge of…a change brought on by social and biological forces that can no longer be ignored or put aside."

As of 2009, Paul Hawken has been awarded six honorary doctorates.

Walt Disney

Mobility Scientist

I look to Disney as a visionary transportation designer. His parks, in general, are mainly designed to move thousands of people each day in the happiest place on earth. Imagine Disney's monorail throughout Southern California and across the country.

Walt Disney was born December 5, 1901 in Chicago's Hermosa community area and died on December 15, 1966. His father, Elias Disney, was Irish Canadian and his mother, Flora Call Disney, was German American.

Walt Disney is well-known for his work in movies and for the many Disneyland theme parks throughout the world. He has been instrumental in providing cherished entertainment to millions over the years, but what he is less known for is his work in imagineering a model community that was years ahead of the culture it was trying to change.

Disney's dream was to build a city—in which he collaborated with Buckminster Fuller—called EPCOT (Experimental Prototype Community of Tomorrow) that would house 20,000 people in such a way, as expressed by E. Cardan Walker, the Disney Chairman and CEO in 1982:

> To all who come to this place of joy, hope and friendship— welcome. EPCOT is inspired by Walt Disney's creative vision. Here, human achievements are celebrated through imagination, wonders of enterprise and concepts of a future that promises new and exciting benefits for all. May EPCOT Center entertain, inform and inspire and above all, may it instill a new sense of belief and pride in man's ability to shape a world that offers hope to people everywhere in the world.

It was Disney's goal to create a model community which would be a test for city planning and organization. It would be built in a circle with the business and commercial areas in the center surrounded by community buildings, schools, and recreational complexes and then surrounded by the residential areas on the outside perimeter. Monorails would have transported people, and all vehicles would be kept underground so that only pedestrians would be on street level.

Disney said of his dream:

> It will be a planned, controlled community, a showcase for American industry and research, schools, cultural and educational opportunities. In EPCOT, there will be no slum areas because we won't let them develop. There will be no landowners and therefore no voting control. People will rent houses instead of buying them, and at modest rentals. There will be no retirees; everyone must be employed.

Disney was a visionary in every sense of the word. Whether it was entertaining and delighting generations of families or behind-the-scenes trying to create a better world, his input and actions will be around for many years to come. Later in his life, he was concerned with improving all life and was trying to provide his idea as a test to its practicality, but he died before he saw any of his ideas fulfilled.

His original version of EPCOT can still be seen in the Magic Kingdom park while riding the Tomorrowland Transit Authority attraction when entering the show house for Stitch's Great Escape. The model is located to the left when facing forward and is behind glass. The funding Disney needed to realize this vision of EPCOT and start work on the Florida property was contingent upon building the Magic Kingdom initially. Unfortunately, he died before the Magic Kingdom opened.

Disney's fascination with life went far beyond simple entertainment. His focus was on the idea of transportation. All his parks were designed with the idea of how to move large amounts of people—experiments, if you will—in the best way possible. The transportation system in Disney parks, such as the monorail, are unique and visionary. He wanted to use these creative systems in cities.

Walt Disney has left a legacy that still carries on today, and with other forward thinkers, he has left a challenge to us all to make life better for everyone on the planet. Others have kept working on his dreams and some of them are coming true. There was so much more to the man that even now it is worth studying and applying some of his futuristic ideas in the world we live in today.

Reset the Game

It is okay to restart the game anytime you like.

If you find yourself in a shipwreck or a plane about to crash, *by all means, save yourself first!* Then as you are secure, look to help someone else. If they try to pull you under? Let them go. This is the art of detachment: the best lifeguard must always ensure their own safety first.

The objective of the WholEarth Game is to find ways to live and travel without harm to this planet or any other living entity. The Game intends to teach you to imagine a future of how to make the world work for 100 percent of all living things in the shortest possible time without further harm or disadvantage to anyone or anything.

Are these extravagant ideas? Currently in our de-evolution, perhaps. We are at the turning point. But there's always a chance to reset the game. Don't give up. Together with whole systems design thinking, we can plant the seed that'll grow into *what happens next.*

Imagine a Future on One WholEarth

The WholEarth System is a compass, a guideline, a standard by which to stay focused on the things that make a complete *whole systems design*. Our goal is making our planet more livable and stopping any future destruction.

Housing, water, food, energy, and occupation make up a whole systems design.

Play with Integrity

Rebuilding a planet is a colossal idea. It will take a lot of *work*. But as we begin to *seed*, the work will turn into fun and games. Don't take yourself too seriously. The journey of a thousand steps starts and ends under your feet.

The WholEarth Game is a game. It was written simply so that we can both have fun and benefit a higher purpose.

I don't know about you but I like making up new words. The word *WholEarth* was designed to draw a clear line of reference to the *Whole Earth Catalogue*. After a chance to hang out and study with J. Baldwin, a teacher on the life and times of R. Buckminster Fuller, I felt inspired to take on this challenge.

I designed WholEarth to make one word out of two. To make a single idea out of what appears on the surface a complicated problem. By bringing these two words together, I hope to convey the fact that we live in a whole system made up of interconnected parts. We are all connected to our planet and each other. The five elements I spoke about earlier are necessary for all life on this planet.

I took it upon myself to help simplify the whole idea.

Water is a fine example of pure integrity. As individual molecules, oxygen and hydrogen are both incredible and are the two basic components that sustain life on earth. However, only together do they make life possible. They are one happy three-way: H2O. There is nothing as fine and as pure as H2O. Pure water has and maintains perfect integrity. As a liquid and a solid, water is the most influential element of the whole planetary system.

What should stay on Spaceship Earth and what must go?

You already know the answer to these questions. The object of the WholEarth Game is to find ways to live and travel without harming yourself, another person, or the planet. You are the ultimate authority in the WholEarth Game.

But first, don't take yourself too seriously. If you fail, you begin the winning process—because you tried. When you win, help someone else win. Always do your best.

Players solve the dilemma of planning for a decent standard of living while protecting the quality of our environment. Students act out the roles of members of a simple economy: producers, consumers, resource developers, and environmental planners. An instructor's manual describes equipment, the time required for the projects, and steps for playing the game.

You've already got what you need. Now *play*.

As you look inside, you might find your own ideas that will lead you to other ideas. You've just got to play. Find happiness in joy and strength in freedom. Keep looking; these are just around the corner.

The WholEarth Game was written to suggest that the world is complete and that everything we need for real and lasting change is at our fingertips. Everything we need to take care of every living thing is—and has always been—available to us for the last 1 billion of the 4.8 billion years that this sphere has occupied space.

Integrity is an interface—an interface to transcend the misinformed impositions of our current cultural story that are directly responsible for our cultures' most vexing problems.

Unfortunately, this reality surfaces far too infrequently in our culture. Our educational system teaches us something vastly different, so we tend to be woefully unprepared to see this reality much less able to think and act in total alignment with universal integrity. The very idea of a game implies that this could be something fun.

The Game may be simple but it takes a lifetime to play. The Game is fun when we are winning, and it allows and encourages everyone to participate. But remember: integrity has no compromise, and compromise has no integrity.

So just what is integrity? The *Merriam-Webster Online Dictionary* defines integrity as:

> 1) firm adherence to a code of especially moral or artistic values: incorruptibility; 2) an unimpaired condition: soundness; 3) the quality or state of being complete or undivided: completeness.

With these definitions in mind, why does integrity matter? Why get more familiar with it? For one reason: it's because integrity is not a casual consideration; it is an operational standard of the universe (and the universe is complete—nothing is missing or left out).

Western culture teaches us that—as humans—we are separate from the universe, but in fact, we are an integral part of its totality. We are not only part of the universe, but we are a result of the universe's perpetual creative drive, living examples of increasing structural complication. We are (so far) our best example of the universe interpreting itself through subjective means. We have no choice about what our inherent relationship with integrity is yet we can choose whether we honor this relationship.

When we truly understand this and increasingly make choices to operate consistently with this integrity, the world changes for the better. We might even begin to question behaviors that make absolutely no sense when viewed in the context of universal integrity and/or when determining what our culture needs to do if we are going to take care of everyone. As Ancient Greek physician Hippocrates wrote, "First, Do No Harm." Although meant for physicians, this can be applied further to how we treat ourselves, each other, and the planet.

This is because the universe operates in absolute integrity according to her governing principles/laws/truths (PLTs), always in dynamic balance, never unprepared, and never unsure of what to do. This is because all PLTs are explainable/discoverable (to humans) as to why they have the effect they do. It is truly a simple *equation*, but there are many moving parts.

The following is a quote from R. Buckminster Fuller, in his book *Operating Manual for Spaceship Earth* published September 1, 1979, by the University of Massachusetts Press. His words underline the omnipresence of integrity:

> The greats have ever been inspired by the
> a priori integrities of Universe and by the need
> of all humanity to move from the absolute igno-
> rance of birth into a little greater understanding
> of the cosmic integrities.

R. Buckminster Fuller loved making up new words to better describe what he was thinking.

Other words he created were:

> *Dymaxion* from the words *dynamic, maxi-*
> *mum* and *ion.* (See also Dymaxion House 1923,
> Dymaxion Car 1933, and Dymaxion Map 1943).
> *Geodesic dome* 1967.
> *Tensegrity* from the words *tension* and
> *integrity.*

When we are truly awake, nature is a terrific model for integrity. We note that no existing species is a failure—all that survive are successes. No species other than ourselves that we are aware of is equipped to make choices other than to comply with natural laws and adapt to changing conditions. When they cannot adapt, they perish.

In a similar light, we have discovered that the operation of gravity (among a plethora of natural laws) is predictable, and therefore, useful and reliable.

Anthropologist Daniel Quinn, in his 1992 book *Ishmael* offers this, "It [a 'universal' law] makes no distinction between human civilizations and beehives. It applies to all species without distinction."

Clearly nothing happens in the world without a direct cause/effect relationship to natural PLTs. Every experience we have humanly is explained through governing universal laws. This is great news because it means that this is an overarching integrity, continually available to each of us, to assist us in making choices as we go through our lives.

In our culture, life tends to move so fast and the demands of merely surviving are so all-consuming that it seems few have time to consider the role that universal integrity might play in their lives—or have time to consider exactly why humans have so many problems when other species pretty much thrive in their niche (that is, until humans come along and mess them up).

Anthropologists tell us it has not always been like this. They report that humans have been on earth for around three million years—mostly living with evolutionary stability—adapting to environmental changes naturally and thriving in a way unlike virtually every other species.

Then around 10,000 years ago, our cultural story took us on a precarious route that began to compromise our inherent integrity. According to Quinn, with the advent of what we call *the agricultural revolution*, a *new* culture began to operate differently choosing to:

1. lock up all the food;
2. operate as if the world was made for man and man was made to dominate;
3. start believing that humans are flawed;
4. start building cities;
5. enable a hierarchical social structure;
6. begin individual ownership of things; and
7. start believing in scarcity as a dominant paradigm.

These significant shifts have proven to be totally out of integrity with the PLTs governing human experience and are major contributors to the peril our culture is currently experiencing.

Our dominating culture has perpetuated this unfortunate, out-of-integrity *game* of attempting to put square pegs in round holes. Plus we have made up all kinds of strange stories to justify or defend what we keep doing to our planet. Apparently the tipping point that puts humans on the brink of self-extinction (the sixth major extinction) is when the human population approaches seven billion. The problem? We are already at seven and a half billion.

As we learn more of what there is to learn about the integrity of being human, we can see that we all come into human experience with the full complement of qualities and characteristics of being human—needing to get nothing externally in order to be more human. Therefore it is clear that we are *evolved* to thrive in our niche like virtually every other species with a similar capability to trust our inherent intuition and/or instincts to enable us to adapt and evolve in an evolutionarily stable manner.

It is totally possible to restore integrity to our cultural paradigms if we simply begin rethinking everything and begin seriously to ask ourselves questions such as, "What makes a concept or idea true?" And/or "What is the governing law?" And requiring the answer to be directly supported by definable universal PLTs.

This could initiate a helpful return to living in integrity and lead to realizing our capability to take care of everyone, to again Do No Harm. If you back up far enough, it becomes clear that virtually all our cultures' most vexing problems would have no place to exist if all our decisions passed through filters of universal integrity.

With Hippocrates in mind, it occurred to me that the ultimate goal of the WholEarth Game is to find ways to live and travel with the least harm.

There is a way to consider and include integrity in virtually every aspect of human life. Here are just a couple of examples: What if we realized that more than seven billion of us (and the entire community of life) are just passengers on a complex spaceship—spaceship earth—turning on our axis at over 1,000 miles per hour and flying around the sun at over 60,000 miles per hour?

In the words of Buckminster Fuller, "That is a whole lot of spin and zip!"

So in actuality, we are all passengers on spaceship earth with all provisions on board (except for the continually arriving energy from the sun). We are totally dependent on these provisions for our life support. No resupply vehicle is expected.

Who in this scenario deserves to control these integral provisions? Who is qualified to take control of any part of the ship? And perhaps, most importantly, who has the right to enjoy a disproportionate amount of our vital provisions at the expense of another equally important passenger? How then does integrity come into play?

Here is another macro example in one of humanity's most prolific activities: construction. Let's look from a different perspective. How does nature build? Buckminster Fuller had the audacity to ask this question and the result was the geodesic dome—a method of enclosing space with the least possible material. Geodesic domes get stronger the greater the span, and they can be built miles in diameter with no internal support.

This technology came about because the triangle is the minimum structure that has structural integrity. Currently the dominant human building method is the square and cube which have no structural integrity until they are triangulated with a brace. Right angles are rarely found in nature.

Let's look at a construction example in a micro sense. What if we approached every industrial process with the integrity inherent in nature? Looking closely, we see that everything in nature is a nutrient for something else. Nothing is ever wasted or becomes *garbage*—every molecule is returned to its basic form to be recycled or reused effortlessly over and over, *ad infinitum*. Is it possible that every human industrial process could be designed in such a manner so that no waste is ever created, and every element is seen as a nutrient for some other process? Wouldn't that be the optimum application of integrity?

These are the type of results we can expect in every area of human experience when we rigorously and intentionally filter everything through the integrity of universal PLTs. And while these examples may be somewhat esoteric, they are intended to stimulate the question, What else can we rethink in new and creative ways? Also the practical application of integrity to one's everyday life has the distinct possibility of uncovering novel ways to overcome the 10,000 years of momentum that has led our culture into the crisis that perpetuates our problems today.

Because of the very nature of integrity, when one constantly makes decisions in alignment, the natural consequence is that lives become less stressful, more joyful, and substantially more fulfilling. Because of the integrity of integrity itself, when we are in greater alignment, excelling at the game of life happens naturally. Learning about and applying integrity truly creates optimum leverage.

This is how we play. We come here to practice and to perfect. As we can never be perfect, we must continue to practice.

Let's Seed What's Happening

We must stop the advance of ecologically unsound practice by preventing its use. As a team, we must let the world know we will not accept it. We will prevent or delay any moves contrary to our objective by using countermoves to negate what our opposition is trying to do. We will even consider the legal environment if necessary.

We must no longer blindly accept the word of the very animal that is destroying the world. We need to band together and do what should have been done years ago had the corporate political animal not taken control of humanity's advancement. It is time to take back our rights and our world and direct it to a place where everyone and everything is taken care of. It's time to realize that most of what you read or hear in the public realm from government or media is misinformation to distract you from the important issues.

Make a stand!

It's obvious that our *leaders* aren't leading, and our situation is just getting worse.

> …this nation, under God, shall have a new birth of freedom; and that government of the people, by the people, for the people, shall not perish from the earth.
>
> —Abraham Lincoln (his closing words of the Gettysburg Address delivered on November 19, 1863.)

Our government is no longer of the people, it's certainly not by the people, and it would be a long stretch to think it's for the people. It's time to reclaim our heritage and recover our government by giving them a loud and clear message about what we are putting together. The path of destruction we're on needs to stop, and it needs to stop now. We don't have much time to correct the greed of those before us and change what the world will be for those who come after us.

The nobility feared the people. And rightfully so. They were demanding three things: housing, clean water, and food.

When the people begged for bread, Marie Antoinette suggested cake.

Tools of the Game

Bucky's Tool Kit

Buckminster Fuller used this as a guideline for whole systems thinking.

Comprehensive, starting from the whole system and working backward to its constituent parts, we seek to deal with all facets of our problem including the larger system the problem is a part of.

Anticipatory, in that it seeks to recognize the threats coming down the pike before they arrive full-blown on an unsuspecting or ill-prepared society as well as to deal with where we are heading and when our solution is going to be implemented.

A design strategy in contradiction to a political or *let's pass the law and change human behavior* approach that seeks to change the larger system of which a specific problem was a part of. A revolution from an individual rather than a collective, regulatory body.

A science-based methodology that utilizes the latest advances in technology and science to benefit all living things.

Toltec Toolkit

Keep a clear conscience.

Another important tool to use while playing the WholEarth Game is the Four Agreements as presented by Don Miguel Ruiz.

Here are the Four Agreements based on an ancient Mayan practice.

1. Always do your best because half measures achieve nothing. Live every day as if it were your last day on One

WholEarth. No regrets. Leave everything on the field. You will be a winner every time.

2. Use kind speech with yourself first. Then, use kind and simple speech with all those around you. Make sure that you understand what you want, then be sure exactly what others expect from you. You both might need to repeat these needs and expectations in a conversation and in writing on important matters.

3. Don't take anything personally. Your dream is only how you can be the best person you can be. Allow others to have their own dreams. Do not interfere with another person's dream. Sometimes, we can dream the same dream and the result can be amazing.

4. Don't make any assumptions without a clear definition of understanding with others. Do your own research. Make your own conclusions. Is this the world you have dreamed of? Is everything in this world right for you and countless others? I ask you to leave this book where another might find it so they, too, can decide whether or not to play the Game. Avoid gossip. Many of us who are not happy use gossip to hurt other people to make us feel better.

The Alcoholics Toolkit

The twelve principles of Alcoholics Anonymous are: honesty, hope, faith, courage, integrity, willingness, humility, self-discipline, love of others, perseverance, spiritual awareness, and service to others.

The primary purpose is to stay focused and to help others achieve focus. In AA we try to practice these principles in all our affairs. We are not saints; no one among us has been able to achieve anything like perfection. Always do your best.

The History of Alcoholics Anonymous

In 1935, a doctor and a businessman decided to use the telephone to help each other. They knew that they had to reach out and help others stay sober. As suggested by both a friend and a physician, the men went to the local hospital trying to find other alcoholics ready to try what they were doing for each other. In those days, people with alcohol addiction were left to just go insane or die.

Very little was known about how to help these seemingly weak-natured and incurable people. Because of this practice, a man who had been diagnosed as chronic had a spiritual awakening. He has been joined by countless others and to this day, millions have been able to recover from alcoholism and many other forms of addiction.

The *Big Book* of Alcoholics Anonymous was written by Dr. Bob Smith and Bill Wilson and the fellowship of Alcoholics Anonymous.

> ALCOHOLICS ANONYMOUS is a worldwide fellowship of countless thousands of alcoholic men and women who banded together to solve their common problems and help fellow sufferers in recovery from that age-old, baffling malady, alcoholism.

This book details how it works. They developed the *Twelve Steps* and the *Twelve Traditions* of Alcoholics Anonymous. It presents an explicit view of the principles by which AA members recover and by which their Society functions. It made me think: *Imagine using this program to help us find a way out of our addiction to oil, coal, and nuclear energy?*

I believe the *Big Book of AA* may be one of the most influential books written in the last century. This work has proven itself for countless thousands to be the clear path away from jails, institutions, and death to a road which promises happiness, joy, and freedom.

From all the searching I have done philosophically—both inwards and outwards—I am able to understand different points of view that lend themselves to my understanding of what is going to happen to the planet. If it could work for a bunch of drunks and drug addicts, why couldn't it work for the planet we call home?

I try my best to practice the principles of AA in all my affairs. I imagine applying the 12-step program to our collective addiction to oil, coal, and nuclear power. These multinational corporations are like the alcoholic parents in the family. Like the alcoholic parent who continues to abuse alcohol while the family is starving around them.

Based on what we know about the pathology of addiction, if left unchecked, these destructive forces will destroy all of us. I suggest we use these steps to understand the foundation of the WholEarth Game. The WholEarth Game is meant to be played on an ever changing pitch. The game should adapt to meet the challenge.

If you feel like you have a problem with food, sex, gambling, or any other thing, you probably do. GET HELP! There is no place in your life for anything that might take you away from being the best person you can be. The twelve steps are the pathway: an easier and softer way to happiness, joy, and freedom.

The WholEarth Game reminds us to stay focused on the big game to save *Gaia*.

We are all addicted to oil, coal, nuclear power, and waste. We are not at fault; we seem to have been born that way. Those in control of our planet have left us no choice. They continue to design and produce unhealthy food and water packaged in various forms that continue to make us sick.

Generally, the rule of thought is that it doesn't matter how you get there as long as you get there. I will add to that point with, "as long as you don't hurt someone or something on the way."

You can mix and match thought or philosophy and put it together to form your own ideology as long as it is used to further what we're all striving for. You will be making your own special blend of thought anyway because it is our nature to react to what we really like and incorporate that into our thought processes. Once we've done that, we approach the task with our own unique and innovative style.

First, we must admit we are addicted to energy. Like any other drug, it is the root cause of most of our current problems. Fossil fuels have been the cause of our disease for the last 150 years. Time to use the inventions of Nikola Tesla to free us from this addiction. The ego will kill the body to protect itself. This ego must be taken down.

Then we come to believe the good works can restore U.S. to sanity.

Next, we need to decide on a personal and collective level to do the right thing. In our hearts we know that we cannot continue to burn fossil fuels and waste our vital natural resources. And yet we still do.

As a world of individuals, we must find a different path. Any business that does not take a regular inventory of what is working and what is not working will go broke. It is time to make tough decisions to find ways to live and travel without harming the planet. We made a searching and fearless inventory of our unsustainable energy practices.

We must admit to ourselves that the old ways will not work. We need to take full responsibility for our actions up to now. We need to be willing to do whatever it takes to restore *Gaia* to her former perfection. We must hold accountable all those businesses and corporations that got us to this point. We need to be willing to face the exact nature of our wrongs. We must be entirely ready to remove all business entities that create harm.

We must humbly become willing to change. We must make a list of living things we have harmed and became willing to make amends to them all. We do this wherever possible except when to do so would cause more harm. We must all have desire to stop using coal, oil, nuclear, and other carbon-based energy; stop making waste.

There is no such thing as waste. There is no place called away. We are simply turning resources from one thing to another thing. When life gives you lemons, make lemonade.

Ecological Design Mandala

This drawing is intended to give you a visual understanding of where we are now and where we need to be. If you look at the Mandala—which was beautifully designed by a student of Professor John Todd—this process encapsulates the real problems we're dealing with today. In the inner circle, where Professor Todd lists the problems beginning in an outward spiral, you will note that he sees the Contemporary Crisis. We are still in the inner circle of the picture. These are the issues that are affecting us right now:

1. Over Consumption
2. Threatened Atmosphere
3. Extinctions
4. Overpopulation

This begins his process to correct the dependence we tend to rely on that vastly undermines the sustainability of our planet. He calls this *The Design Revolution* and lists four beginning steps to get us on the road of repair:

1. The need for design revolution
2. Setting up the new books
3. Ecological footprints
4. Radical perception shift

Now following his design into the next outward spiral, he lists eight factors for starting the process of reclaiming the earth:

1. Precepts for ecological design
2. Overview of the Seven Schools of ecological design
3. New Alchemy: The Necessary Synthesis
4. Microcosms
5. The Properties of Water
6. Runaway CO2/NOX Universe
7. Comparative Models; plant, animal, whale
8. Algal Scrubbers

Again having listed certain properties to begin the process, he takes it a step further in his next group by listing what can be seen as practical application and lessons taught from nature:

1.   Coral reefs as models for design
2.   The Maine coast as a model
3.   Florida Mangroves as a model
4.   Eel grass communities as teachers
5.   Space colonies
6.   Biosphere II: lessons learned
7.   The emergence of living machines
8.   12 Principles of design

The outer ring of the mandala shows the solutions and how we, as a concerned species, can implement programs that will allow for natural regrowth of our planet's natural resources. By instituting these listed procedures, growth and sustainability can be achieved:

1.   Living machines and restorers at work; which include— restoration, waste conversion, food production and new products
2.   Ecological Aquaculture
3.   Living on the water
4.   Farms, forests, and reinhabiting the rural landscape
5.   Urban farms and ecology in the city
6.   Ecological industrial parks, bio mimicry and the transformation of manufacturing
7.   Redesigning the campus and community
8.   The rise of an ecological economy and culture

This is a critical view and assessment of the deficiency we have built into our living arrangement that is not feasible for continued survival in the way we live. Professor Todd is one of many who have had the insight to see where our actions are leading us as our ecological world breaks down around us. As his diagram shows, there are some serious problems we are propagating that need unique and definable solutions.

This work was done some time ago, so the urgency of sustainable behavior is even more prevalent today than it was some twenty or thirty years ago. If enough people get involved in their own part of the world, major change can be implemented, and the slow process of changing the existing ecology can begin. As with many causes, most think the answer is too big for them to do anything about yet any movement starts with one small step leading to bigger and faster growth and, therefore, we play the game.

The WholEarth system is here to help show what needs to be done, and how to reasonably do it. This booklet identifies situations and offers solutions. As with any solution-oriented process, this will not be the end-all for how to fix our problems. New technology is always on the horizon, and once this becomes a cause for the world, technology will adjust to focus more on ecological solutions to help expedite integrating new world information useful to winning the battle against ecological degradation.

The easy part has been done. We've identified the problems and came up with solutions. Now we must get the word out, and get a largely inactive mass of people to learn just how much they can accomplish with one small step if given the right information and understanding necessary to further the promotion of smart, ecological decision-making. Using sustainable methods for living not only makes sense, it will save the planet we're living on and hold in trust for those yet to come.

Again, I am going to remind you what we at WholEarth believe the hierarchy of imperatives is; Housing, Clean Water, Pure Foods, Natural Energy, and Occupation. Briefly, we need these imperatives to be inculcated into our lives, so we can live in harmony and sustainably within the only boundaries we have around us.

I hope you can see how the WholEarth system can take the mystery out of the thing we call sustainability. I hope you can see how this system can be applied to the abject poverty that is one of the most prevalent issue in the world right now. How, by using simple common sense and your grandmother's wisdom, we may again live in a world that provides everything for all living things.

Somehow, we find ourselves at a place where 90% of the people on this planet have inadequate shelter. They dream of clean water, bountiful food, which often they get only once a week, and maybe, if they are lucky, jobs. And the other 10% of us throw away more food than we can eat. These are the imperatives of the WholEarth system: housing, water, food, energy, and occupation. These elements are provided by this planet every day for all living things.

The Great Deception

Fear, shame, guilt, and doubt are the cause of our dis-ease.

In 1949, Eric Blair wrote the book *1984* published under the pseudonym, George Orwell. *1984* was the playbook of the *elite* that would have us enslaved to this day. In the book he coined the term Big Brother. This has become the smartphone you are now addicted to. The now infamous *Orwellian* story is set in London and is about how the country is run by an oligarchical dictatorship. Although the premise is put in fictional settings after an endless global war, Orwell expressed his fear of where the English government is headed currently.

Orwell's story portrays a world of continuous wars, omnipresent government surveillance, and continual public mind control that subordinates the individual to the state. In this manner, The Party (as the controlling government entity is called) controls and manipulates the populace.

In fact, from this novel the term *Orwellian* was coined and used to refer to any organization that uses lies, surveillance, and subtle manipulation of past events to garner support and/or fear to further a totalitarian agenda.

So what do we have today? A government that lies, has engaged in (what was once considered unconstitutional) the monitoring of private citizens, a particularly onerous spin on past facts, and methods to manipulate the majority of people. This is carried out to promote fear and elicit tacit approval so that people need the government to step in and *protect* them. So now, the country is run by a small group that controls all the economic and social morals, and if you don't accept this *new protective government,* you are labeled *unpatriotic.*

The populace accepts this premise with minimal fuss, and now the country is in free fall because the very government that promised to take care of its citizens is controlled by corporate greed. The Corporate Political Animal has reared its ugly head and taken control of the country.

The influence corporations have on our political members runs deep, and the focus has shifted from taking care of the needs of the country's citizens to one of padding the corporate coffers. We are continually at war for questionable reasons, lied to about these wars, had our civil rights reduced, are controlled by corporate manipulated media, and given little or no voice in the future of the country.

The world's ecology is being destroyed in the name of *progress* which at this time is just another name for corporate profit, and it's sanctioned by our very own government. Our government is supposed to serve its people. Common sense has been misplaced as decisions made about the future sustainability of this planet are ignored. Mother Nature is on the edge of the cliff, struggling to hold on.

There is a conflict in thought about what is happening to our planet, and there is still a lot that requires discussion, but the writing is on the wall for our planet's deteriorating health. Similar to what Orwell warned in *1984*, "Big Brother is watching you." Every time you open your cell phone and enter your pin, you are inviting Big Brother further into your life.

It might be about this time that you realize the we live on a prison planet. What *Gaia* provided freely to every living thing has been turned into profit centers for the .001 percent.

Problem

> "Problems cannot be solved with the same
> mindset that created them."
>
> —Albert Einstein

We are currently caught in a cycle of overpopulation, overconsumption, threatened atmosphere, and mass extinction. This is the problem caused by 200 years of the industrial revolution that has benefited 1% of the human population of the entire planet. This is the absolute definition of unsustainable living practice. This is a result of what is labelled Free Market Capitalism.

This is a lot to be concerned about. If you are alive on One WholEarth you should be afraid. But fear is not our guide. Fear keeps us from action and is the biggest lie we tell ourselves.

Isn't that ridiculous? We are all going to win the WholEarth Game. As with anything, we must practice. Failure is as good a teacher as success. Halfway up the ladder nothing is certain. We are most steady with both feet on the ground.

Look at any building, city, town, or neighborhood. Are they producing food, clean water, or energy? If it doesn't have one of those three things, then it is not going to work. If it does not include the WholEarth system, then the chances are that they're not good for the people.

Capitalism is a waste-driven program: waste human energy, waste material goods and services. However, there is no such thing as waste! Mostly the things we see on the streets today are petroleum-based products, coal, oil, nuclear. 90% of all things made with plastic are designed to be thrown away. Right now, we don't have any control over it. When you are only given bad choices, it is impossible to make a good decision.

"Everybody knows the poor get poor and the rich get rich. There's a meter on your head, that's how it goes, everybody knows."
—Leonard Cohan

Solution

"We could change the world tomorrow if all the
millions of people around the world acted the
way they believe."

—Jane Goodall

By combining the elements of the WholEarth system (housing, water, food, energy, and occupation) with the principles of *Natural Capitalism*, i.e.…resource productivity, service and flow, biomimicry, and reinvestment of wealth, we can achieve the results we need to achieve. This is our best chance to build the best possible future and win this game together.

Many will scoff at the idea that we can save this planet from complete destruction. But as we begin to change our ways, the earth will rapidly begin the healing process. It is possible for people from all backgrounds to live together in respect for each other and in respect for the place we call home.

We want to change mankind's environment for the benefit of all. No more starvation, no more waterborne diseases, no more poverty, and no more energy that leaves a negative footprint. This and the ability for all to provide for themselves and others. First, we must imagine this; secondly, we must implement this.

How are we going to do this? Am I out of my mind? Maybe, but we as a species did it successfully for hundreds of thousands of years before the Industrial Revolution changed the way we lived.

I'm not advocating a return to a *hunter/gatherer* way of life. I'm suggesting we implement a program that proposes societal unity. This is a program where everyone will work toward a common goal.

Simply put: it means changing the way we live to promote healthy living for all of us as well as the land, water, air, and everything else that we are a part of. We must provide communities across the world the knowledge of how to become self-sustainable in a complete reorientation of how we live. A movement, if you will, to teach all of us how to live in congruence with everything around us.

Anticipate the Game

To know your enemy is to know yourself.

It is imperative to make a simple plan and stick to it. Find ways to live and travel without harming yourself or anything else. Now! Stay focused and help others to stay focused.

Remember: will all need just five things.

1. a place to sleep
2. clean pure fresh water
3. good food
4. energy
5. an occupation/stuff to do

First, get these for yourself. Then help others get these five things and that is about it.

I truly believe that through thoughtful design, we can improve the lives of millions of people around the world. I believe that if we combine the knowledge of the past with the technology of today, not only could we improve the lives of people but we could also make those lives as enjoyable as possible.

I intend to approach the problem of housing and community differently in each instance. I believe that in most cases, the people already know what they need. What they don't know was how to get and use the technology available to them that could improve their situation.

As a designer, I am a problem-solver. With research and experimentation, we can all find a solution.

With the WholEarth system of building, we can produce quality, affordable homes with less time and less energy than anything currently being used. No person should be without basic shelter, clean water, and healthy food. The system puts building back into the hands of the people where it all began.

To understand the problem, you must first look at it from all sides. Then you can start to design a *new way*. The fundamental idea is to use historical and preindustrial models to bring change and economic growth to the people of the future.

Instead of always looking to invent something new and different, it is possible to take what we need from the past. We can use technology and ideas that worked well for ten thousand years rather than technology that has been failing the planet for the last two hundred years.

In 1995, I woke up, knowing that we were living unsustainably. We cannot continue to grow in the ways those who are leading us demand. Many of the world's cities are overcrowded and filled with people who don't have jobs, money, food, or proper sanitation.

On any given night on television, in newspapers, and in magazines, you can find articles telling of the poverty and despair throughout the world. Here in the United States, people are suffering from the lack of essential needs. But this is a global crisis.

The idea is to put power back into the hands of the people at the local level and to stop allowing a government or corporate entity take all the power. People need to learn how to take control of their own lives again. By looking back at preindustrial models of community organization and the ability to control basic needs, much could be done to improve their quality of life on a local level. We must continually stress the basic and common needs of all people: housing, water, food, industry, and energy.

About the Author

Alanson Jared Charles

I was always just a bench sitter, really; always wanted to play on the first string. But for the most part, I like to practice by myself quietly. Waiting for my chance.

But the game isn't over, and I still have a lot to share. For whatever reason, I was given a complete download as to how to fix a planet. Take it or leave it. I'm just here to show you what I'm thinking. You are here to make it happen.

I was born in Yonkers, New York, and given the name David Laurence Bowman. In 1961, when I was six months old, I was adopted by Raymond Alanson Charles and Lois Sokora Charles. I was given the name Alanson Jared Charles.

My folks Ray and Lois were super smart and loved me as much as any people could. I had the best possible life growing up. And having been so blessed, it is only right to give back as much as possible to those who have less.

I am a child of the world.

I attended a private school in Morristown, New Jersey, and graduated in 1978. Although I was an average student, I was able to paint and draw. After graduating, I attended New England College. Shortly after, I transferred to U.C.S.B and graduated with a BA in letters and science.

U.C.S.B was—and still is—an inspiration as it is a great example of ecological and architectural design. Once they add the food component in order to feed their students, they will be complete.

I graduated in 1983, and after, I worked on building homes and driveways in Santa Barbara until 1995.

I was given a business card in 1989 with no name or number on it. It merely said, "Dream Large Dreams, Because Small dreams have no power to inspire." That night I had a dream. I was visited and told, "Help as many people as possible in the short amount of time left on this planet. If you build it, they will come."

I believe that my creator spoke to me with a clear message. It was revealed to me that I was here to help as many people as possible find a home. I was here to build a lifeboat. As one small person filled with fear, guilt, shame, and doubt, what could I do?

I asked, "Why me?"

They said, "Why not you?"

In 1993, I designed the Eco Tube House. This house can be produced on an assembly line at the rate of one home every 30 minutes. That would equate to 17,520 per year with one machine. With ten machines running 24hours a day, that would equate to 175,200 per year. While using the least amount of energy, time, material, and labor we can build as many as we need. The Pacific Roller Die machine is small and lightweight. It can be replicated to meet whatever need.

I applied to Art Center College of Design in Pasadena with a business plan to build the eco tube house wherever people needed a house. I was accepted.

On January 16, 1995, the same day that my son Joseph was born, I began my journey at Art Center and thus, WholEarth was born.

While a student at Art Center College of Design 1995–98, I created the WholEarth system to express my passion and commitment to whole system design strategies. I learned to use less and waste none and was finding ways to live and travel without harm.

While attending school, I was introduced to many other low-cost building systems that could be used to help others. Earth and straw-bale, building with trash. I was introduced to the men who were early bioneers, as presented earlier. The Eco Tube House was only one of many ways to provide a safe place to sleep with healthy natural materials.

At school I discovered my true nature. I am a visionary. I see things that are missing. I want them to be there. A wayseer. I live to show others the way. I am an anticipatory design science generalist. I keep an open mind. I love people of all ages. They are all me; I am all of them. I want them to have the best possible future. I want the best possible future. My personal goal is to be the best person I can be and help others to do the same.

I called Diaky to ask what I could do. I started going into all the ideas I had that might work to improve the lives of the people there. At one point she said, "Stop, Lance! All the things you are telling me sound great. You need to write a book."

I said, "A book?"

Another roadblock, but when the spirit provides a clear answer, I just go along to see what's going to happen.

She told me that if I wanted to be taken seriously, I needed to start writing. And if I wanted her help in promoting my ideas, the book had to be completed by the Eighth Annual Artivist Film Festival.

I'm happy to report that I finished the rough draft one week before the Festival. On October 30, 2011. I was able to hand out 100 copies of the first addition of this book at Occupy L.A. on November 11, 2011, or 11.11.11.

I might have been the only person to realize that we were there to reset the WholEarth Game.

I believe that the creator had spoken to me during a coma caused by a work-related accident and a near-death experience in late 1989. I received a clear message from a voice inside me. I was being officially initiated into the Federation of Galactic Light Workers. It was revealed to me that I was here to help as many people as possible and to build a lifeboat. I was here to help others.

Prior to the fall, I had been battling in my brain about how to provide quality affordable housing and to positively affect the lives of as many people as possible in the time I have left here on this earth.

After the fall, I was committed.

This path led me to one of the finest design schools in the world: Art Center College of Design, class of 1998. That experience allowed me to meet some of the most active and important people in the field of sustainability. I have met and worked with people who might end up being the most influential for the future of our country and the rest of the world. You just never know. I might be one of them too.

Just before Easter 2010, another stranger sent me a link to the Wayseers Manifesto. It was a video montage of an idea: that all of us misfits and troublemakers were really those who were the catalysts of real change. I felt at home after seeing that video, rushed to join Wayseers, and met Garret John LoPorto online.

Garret and the Wayseers allowed me to discover I was not only a DaVinci Mind, but in fact a Super DaVinci Mind. Though I can't really draw, I do have the ability to see a project, object, and a construct in a *completed* way. I was encouraged at Wayseers to think this way. I am a Wayseer, soon to be a Wayshower.

Encouraged and motivated by Wayseers and Diaky, I began writing the WholEarth Game in January 2011. Inspired by the book *Blessed Unrest*, I wanted to present my ideas in the context of a game. The infinite game. The game we play to live. The game we play to laugh. The game we play to love.

I must mention that underneath all the information and subject matter of this book are years of listening to my favorite free speech radio stations, KPFK 90.7 FM and KPFK.org. It is a plain fact that this book would not be possible without the information so freely given by the great folks at KPFK.

The knowledge of the world I gained by listening to the radio station gave me the direction and focus I needed while attending Art Center College of Design in Pasadena. Those who come to mind from the radio station are Terrence McNally, Amy Goodman, Sonali Kolhatkar, Roy of Hollywood, Alan Watts, Maria Armoudian, Christine Blosdale, Alan Minski, Jerry Quickley, Margaret Prescod, Lila Garret, Caroline Casey, Don Bustany, Jim Lafferty, Suzi Weissman, Mitch Jeserich, Michael Slate, and so many more. It would be impossible to name them all.

Without this knowledge so freely given by KPFK, these ideas—and subsequently this book—would not exist.

Eco tube housing. Quality housing that's fast and affordable.

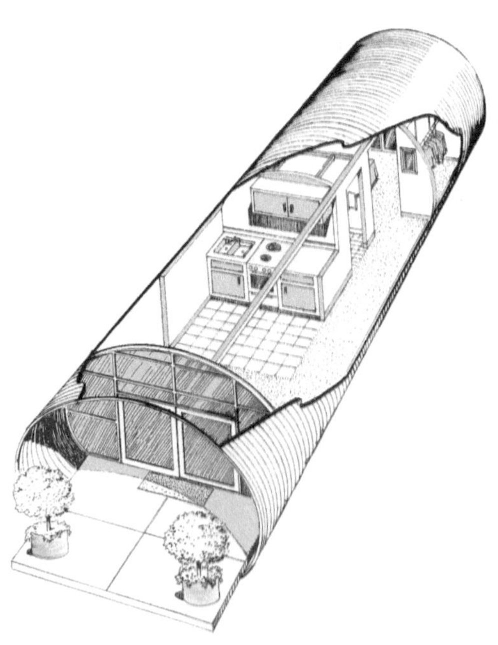

www.ingramcontent.com/pod-product-compliance
Lightning Source LLC
Chambersburg PA
CBHW031418250726
48656CB00002B/721